D0064859

GHOST VOLCANO

GHOST VOLCANO

poems by

Sandra M. Gilbert

W. W. NORTON & COMPANY

NEW YORK / LONDON

The text of this book is composed in Weiss
with the display set in Bernhard Tango and Weiss.
Composition by Crane Typesetting Service, Inc.
Manufacturing by The Courier Companies, Inc.
Book design by JAM DESIGN.

Library of Congress Cataloging-in-Publication Data

Gilbert, Sandra M.
Ghost volcano : poems / by Sandra M. Gilbert.
      p.   cm.
      I. Title.
    PS3557.I34227G48   1995
  811'.54—dc20   94–45910

ISBN 0-393-03783-5

W.W. Norton & Company, Inc., 500 Fifth Avenue, New York, N.Y. 10110
W.W. Norton & Company Ltd., 10 Coptic Street, London WC1A 1PU

1 2 3 4 5 6 7 8 9 0

In memory of Elliot Lewis Gilbert
December 1, 1930—February 11, 1991

A Note to the Reader

On February 11, 1991, my husband, Elliot Gilbert, died following routine surgery at the medical center associated with the university where we both taught. Elsewhere, in a memoir entitled *Wrongful Death*, I tell the story of the circumstances surrounding this event. Here, I collect the poems that I found myself writing in memory of him as I also worked on my prose account. With the exception of a prefatory poem that is slightly out of chronological order, the "Widow's Walk" poems, which appear throughout the book, form a narrative of the stages of grief that I was struggling through in this period. I conceive of "Kissing the Bread," "Notes on Masada," "Water Music," and "Calla Lilies" as more formal elegiac works.

Contents

I. WIDOW'S WALK   15

   October 6, 1992: Seattle, Looking for Mount Rainier   17

II. KISSING THE BREAD   19

   1. and the fields inside it   21
   2. My mother in the four by seven   22
   3. No. No doubt   23
   4. They were kissing the corn god, you say?   24
   5. But no again: my mother's kiss   25

III. WIDOW'S WALK   27

   October 26, 1991: Outside Saratoga Springs   29
   October 29, 1991: 4 PM, outside Saratoga Springs   30
   December 21, 1991: Berkeley Solstice   31
   January 30, 1992: On the Beach at Santa Barbara   32
   February 11, 1992: At the Art Institute of Chicago   34
   April 17, 1992: The Good Friday Spell, by the Pacific   36
   May 3, 1992: On the Surface   38
   May 15, 1992: On the Road Again, 101 N,   40
      Listening to C & W
   May 22, 1992: Wagner's Birthday   42
   June 11, 1992: Nursing Home, Framingham, Mass.   44
   June 15, 1992: Widow's Walk, Harpswell, Maine   46

IV. NOTES ON MASADA   49

   1. All night, every night, those old stones   51
   2. In a battered Volvo, driving through the German   53
      Colony
   3. We poke through the 2000-year-old storerooms   54
   4. I confess: I hate religion   55
   5. The head of the eggplant cracks open   56

Contents

6. We quarrel in our California kitchen, eating porkchops   57

7. By the Dead Sea, its turquoise scales   58

8. I'm not who I am. Bless you!   59

9. Beyond the archaic bathhouse, the storage room, the   60

10. And what about the mysteries of Cana?   61

11. What about, as our son put it, *the absolute*   62

12. The shadows of the Church   63

13. Mount Scopus. A lavish lunch at the university   64

V. *WIDOW'S WALK*   67

September 5, 1992: New Hampshire, under the Woods   69

September 7, 1992: Labor Day in the Woods, outside Peterborough   70

September 10, 1992: Picking Wildflowers in New Hampshire   71

November 26, 1992: Thanksgiving at the Sea Ranch, Contemplating Metempsychosis   73

VI. WATER MUSIC   75

1. The Nature of Water   77

2. The Water Goddess   79

3. The Character of Water   81

4. The Ice Cubes   83

5. Hard Water   85

6. Brine   87

7. The Water Table   89

8. The Lake   90

9. Rain   91

VII. *WIDOW'S WALK*   93

March 14, 1993: Berkeley: Trying Not to Think of a White Bear   95

Contents

March 22, 1993: Puerto Vallarta, Sierra Madre/Baya   97
de Los Banderos

Spring Equinox, 1993: Puerto Vallarta, Playa de Los   98
Muertos

VIII. CALLA LILIES   101

IX. *WIDOW'S WALK*   105

December 1, 1993: Paris, Looking at Monet   107

February 11, 1994: Berkeley, Anniversary Waltz Again   109

February 14, 1994: At the Point Reyes Lighthouse   111

Acknowledgments

"Notes on Masada" originally appeared in *The Ontario Review*. "Water Music" was first published in *Poetry*.

For special encouragement, advice, and support with this project, I am grateful to Chana Bloch, Jane Cooper, David Gale, Susanna Gilbert, Susan Gubar, Philip Levine, Diana O'Hehir, Peter Dale Scott, Ruth Stone, Phyllis Stowell, and Alan Williamson.

I

WIDOW'S WALK

October 6, 1992: Seattle, Looking for Mount Rainier

The housekeeper says she doesn't know.
Limping, gray-haired, dwarfed, she's cleaned these rooms
for fifteen years, but she's still not sure.

Over there—she points to a cutout line of hills—
the Olympics maybe.
                        An hour later,

it surges out of the clouds, mystic as Valhalla,
just opposite the spot
where she thought perhaps I'd find it.

Three months after you died, Susan and I
flew over the gasp of the peak
in a tiny frightening Cessna.

I forgot the lacy petals in the meadows outside
Paradise Lodge where we picnicked
en famille in 1980.

Stared at the grooved grim face.
My husband's face, I told her. Dead
and gigantic and frozen in reproach.

Ten minutes wide, centuries long.
I wanted to fall, I was falling, I had fallen
into the hissing crevices, the lanes of ice

where I knew you wandered, shivering
even in your Irish sweater, your old blue parka.
No end to the scowl of the mountain that was you,

no end to the screech of the Valkyrie,
dragging you past the ledges of light
into yourself.

Now,
distant as our innocent goodbye,
it's a mirage on the horizon:

ghost volcano.
Dwellers in this city
say *sometimes you see it,*

sometimes you don't.

II

KISSING THE BREAD

▲   ▲   ▲

Kissing the Bread

1.

and the fields inside it.
The winter of the crumb, the iron
hoe hacking the furrow,
the hiss of grain in the wind.

The priest in the crust
says *kiss*, says
In nomine Domini,
bless, *kiss*.

2.

My mother in the four by seven
yellow kitchen in Queens,
pressing her lips to half a
loaf of day-old challah, the food
of someone else's sabbath,
before dropping it into the silver
step-on can:
her mother the Sicilian midwife
taught her, taught all nine,
to kiss the bread before you
throw it away.

       Why?
Non so. You kiss it, like
crossing yourself before a crisis, before
the train leaves the station,
before the baby falls,
startled, into a sudden
scorch of air.

3.

No. No doubt
not that. But instead
Dickinson's "the Instead."
They were full of terrible
accurate sentiment,
those old Italian ladies in the kitchen—
crones, with witch hairs haloing
their chins, with humps and staggers
and nodes of bone ringing their fingers.

Kissing the bread was kissing
the carrion that was the body
of every body, the wrist

of daughter and husband, the crook'd
arm of the mother, the stone
fist of the father.

Kissing *goodbye*,
saying the daily
goodbye, the skeptical
god be with you
as the long loaf sank into ashes,
as the oven sputtered its
merciless complaint.

4.

They were kissing the corn god, you say?
Kissing the host, the guest,
the handsome one who grows
so tall and naked
in the August grove?

But what if they were mocking him,
mocking the crust that stiffened, the crumbs
that staled and scattered?

> *You thought,*
> *bread, that your magic*
> *salts were eternal, that your holy*
> *taste was your final shape,*
> *but see, you were wrong:*
> *I bid you goodbye, my tongue*
> *gives you a last touch, my teeth*
> *renounce you.*

5.

But no again: my mother's kiss
was humble, the mortified
kiss of guilt—*I can use you
no longer*—and the kiss
of dread: *what will I do, challah,
pumpernickel, rye, baguette, sweet white,
thick black, when you
are gone?*

      And the kiss, I think
I thought she meant,
of sorrow, as if kissing
the bread is kissing
the crows that fly low over
fields we never saw in Queens,
the blurry footprints
between long rows of wheat,
the blank sun roaring overhead.

We stood in the Jackson Heights kitchen.
The white 1940s Kelvinator
whirred, no comment, and strips of
city snow crisscrossed the window.

I was eight and baffled.

*If an angel should be flying by
when you make that face,* she said,
you'll be stuck with it forever.

III

WIDOW'S WALK

October 26, 1991: Outside Saratoga Springs

Unseasonable heat, as I slip toward
Eastern Standard time, below a rank of rusting
east coast trees not far from where
six years ago we quarreled, kissed, gave thanks.

Sun cooks a small polluted pond
you'll never see, coated with curled-up
leaves the local sculptor wants to use
as models for her "floating baskets."

The water's dense and black, as if this lake were
what they call a *tarn;* the trees
lean in, companionably blackening themselves.
Back home, in burnt-out Oakland, an older widow

asked if I "felt a presence."
No I don't. I always hated Halloween,
the fat dead pumpkin with its silly mask
of life, the kids pretending to be ghosts,

the mockery of skeletons. Down here
among the shredded leaves, the rocks are only
rocks, the shreds just shreds,
and the fish that leap in the murk

probably don't know they're "leaping."
Your eyes are gone that might have loved
the last quick lights in these Berkshire trees.
Something turned you into a stone of yourself.

What baskets of wishes
can I imagine fashioning
to float next week across
the chilling waters of All Souls Night?

October 29, 1991: 4 PM, outside Saratoga Springs

My shadow, facing east, is twice my size,
a long dull path through glittering, frost-bitten
blades of grayish green. A hasty glaze
of cold October sun gives it a sudden outline,
and there, on the chilly ground, I guess I am,
a thinning blurring shape that might be a woman
with a walking stick (no, really a cane) and a dim
sort of knob at the top—a head, if it's human!

I move, and this vague road slides forward too,
weaving a little as I do, trying to hide
under dragging branches, shadow under shadow,
then in a clearing pulling into the lead
as if to prove that at this late hour I have
nothing to track but the dark drift of myself.

December 21, 1991: Berkeley Solstice

"The full moon, called by Native Americans the moon of the
long night, occurs tonight."

—*San Francisco Chronicle*, Dec. 21

Low on the horizon,
leaning on the hills,
the moon of the long night
silences the sky:

       its bare
pure white, its great Platonic
circle, seem to dare me
to reach, to try to touch,

as if by touching I might enter
that famous tube of light
through which the near-dead pass into—
into what they cannot know.

"The light is kind," says my grief book.
"The light is good. Those who have seen this light
don't fear it."
       The long night

laps me in shivers, its winds
and tides are rising, its moon
shrinks in the slow climb
toward midnight.

       O you who have entered
the faithless tunnel,
you are farther away
than that small moon.

January 30, 1992: On the Beach at Santa Barbara

Thin and milky, the edges of the sea
swirl toward me, and I in my city blues,
ready for a quick shopping trip,
I with my walking stick, my black
thick widowed shoulder bag,
alighted on this ruinous damp sand
like a gull or a darker migrant bird. . . .

A year ago today in Sacramento they started
to kill you, whoever they were or are.
The ice-white light of the O.R.
stared down at your sprawl, your
tenderness, the naive hair
on your body, your pink
abandoned tongue, your useless beard.

My girls and I were shopping:
the surgeon said to leave, "distract yourselves."
Now, down here, the oil rigs, the yachts, the trawlers
seem to me to hang like relics of another
world beyond the fretting surf,
becalmed on some bizarre gray tissue
that blurs into a sullen sky.

Vicious as needles, sand flies
nip at my calves, my arms.
Can I buy a new life at Nordstrom's?
At least a different bag to tote this sorrow?
In my dream last week we walked together
into the O.R.,
and I told you you would have to die.

You were shocked and scared.

GHOST VOLCANO

But look! I've planted my stick in
the salt and sand of the sea-border,
beside the weeds the Pacific cast away this year.
And I'm stupidly searching the sky for your eyes,
waiting for you here in Santa Barbara,
still speaking to you, still speaking
to what you were.

February 11, 1992: At the Art Institute of Chicago

The Van Gogh roomscape draws me
with its caked and screaming yellow bed,
and then, two yards away, the bloodied eyes
of his devilish self-portrait—

but I pause, instead, in your honor
(wanting to think only of the you you were)
before *Sunday Afternoon at the Grande Jatte*:
those bourgeois ghosts so primly posed

beside a silent stream,
                    and I think
how easily I see clear through them,
they're only shadows

with portentous dogs and bustles
whispering across a phantom light
that rises like swamp fever
from the Grand Jatte's golden ground. . . .

My dear one, my other self, you lay
bleeding to death
in a white chaos where they wouldn't
let us see you: tubes and clicking things,

fearful voices of the Code Team—
trache, pacemaker, transfusions—
and what brilliance of the past
leaped from the ghastly tiles (did any?)

to recall you to the shadow
life on the Grande Jatte,
how we and Seurat studied for it,
sketching the couple over and over, their

GHOST VOLCANO

arm-in-arm silence, their odd
placidity, and the trembling
radiance that blurred behind them
as they stood themselves, unconscious,

in an eerie shade a whole lot
scarier than Van Gogh's scream.

April 17, 1992: The Good Friday Spell, by the Pacific

Blue fangs open in the meadow.
Circles and circles of wild iris,
each the shade of some heroic eye.

Their underground hands—black strings—
cling to my muddy Reeboks
as the bulbs quicken:

they're going to shape more enchanted rings,
and more and more, until
the petals sicken of it all.

You'd say, I know, that such magic
was what Parsifal saw,
the Holy Fool,

trudging through the fields into surprise,
and toward the sad king's wound that bled and bled
unceasingly. . . .

When you were alive, you listened
with all your body, said our son
(as you lay astonished in your coffin).

Good Friday, and all day the radio reiterates
the Wagner that you loved,
and I speak my piece

over and over in my head
by the chill Pacific,
and over again spell out the hopeless words—

GHOST VOLCANO

My love, you're another
bulb down there,
the only blood that's left us

the blue blood of the irises
that spring from the blue tweed jacket
we buried you in

and from the azure peacock eyes
inscribed on your funereal fin-de-siècle
Liberty tie.

May 3, 1992: On the Surface

it's yellow-green, yellow and green
and blue and warm,

and the outlook
for tomorrow is the same:

rhododendrons blooming purple, oleanders
on the freeways, people

strolling on Solano
and people drinking beer

on decks and in cafés
here and there

on Telegraph or Shattuck, and people
rioting, yes darling, in L.A.,

as though this were 1789 or something,
and the president's complaining

although on the surface
it's still

quite still and mild with a smell
of orange blossom rising

(pittosporum said the botanist
I met last week)

and there's the anthropologist who also
wrote to me last week, he says

it's hot in Jersey too plus
evil's in our genes, he's

GHOST VOLCANO

sure of it, there was a talk on this
(his book was central) at the Smithsonian

and I thought him cute
though rather short

but on the surface, here,
it's getting, every day,

a little bluer,
hotter—earthquake weather, some would say—

but on the surface, certainly,
the oaks are pollinating, sexual and yellow,

yellow-green,
and the kids are fine, too, really,

even if down there this new
warmth hasn't trickled through

to you
and it's so dull, I know,

and I suspect
nothing touches what's inside the silent

boxes, nothing creeps into the heaviness
that covers all of you

except the bulbs, the dreadful bulbs exploding
everywhere and rising

toward the surface
through this season's placid grass.

May 15, 1992: On the Road Again, 101 N, Listening to C & W

The little towns unwind their troubles,
twangin' out loneliness,
bangin' out pain.

How she felt, if he'd a known
he'd a been on the telephone,
now he's all alone,

all all alone,
revvin' his Chevy
past that ole Georgia pine.

I turn the sorrow up, tune it sharper:
grandma told grandpa she'd always love him,
but she went on ahead and now she's waitin',

O yes she's waitin' for him to join her,
join her when his chores are done,
join her 'neath the Georgia pine.

The freeway speeds me onward like a mad
trottoir roulant;
                    something—

smog or tears?—fogs up the windshield.
How you would have loathed
this whine of banjos!

Ventura County line. I step on the gas,
hit down hard on the rental Mazda.
I'm plunging ahead, plummeting forward,

away from the dirt back roads
where wan lost lovers spin in their pickups,
lamenting, lamenting.

GHOST VOLCANO

I've set my cruise control and O my love
I'm steering by unknown stars,
aimed for the true deep north

where it's never sad, never warm,
not like here, not like home,
and I believe you're waiting, waiting,

waiting for me to come.

May 22, 1992: Wagner's Birthday*

Parsifal is born today, and today
Tristan begins to die,
and as I know you know

today the innocent sword
will rise from the tree, and the sad king's
wound begin to bleed.

Today, we leap into *leitmotiv*,
today the master singers gather
on the horizon, today Tannhaüser

forsakes himself for Venus,
                              today
the birth of the first opera you'll hear:

now your Russian grandma can order the limo
and sweep you off, twelve years old,
to the Met and the enthralling

Flower Maidens, and the Grail
is born today,
the great gong hollowing the ground

below Broadway so that today
you can resolve that when you finally
find me

we'll go to Bayreuth, watch the sacred
ruler die, and picnic in the intermission—
Schloss Johannisberger, leberkäse, brötchen, fraises des bois—

*Wagner was born on Saturday, May 22, 1813.

GHOST VOLCANO

and after your blood runs out,
almost two centuries from today,
after the gurney like a swan boat

sails you toward the morgue,
I'll wander for days and years
through the grottoes of Amfortas's sorrow,

begging for transformation.

June 11, 1992: Nursing Home, Framingham, Mass.

What is it that goes on living, that goes on
looking out at the flat sheen
of the corridors, the useless twigs

of wrists, the paper
cups of juice? What is it
that mutters under the dry tongue,

through teeth like gravel, like birdseed?
As if she finally faced the demons
at the throat of hell,

my Aunt Francesca, 97 in March
and shrunk to the size of the 9-year-old
bones she came to America in,

stares from her giant wheelchair at the two crones
who guard the door to the elevator
in their own enormous, braked-down chairs.

One shouts, over and over,
*What is in the black soup, what
is in the black soup?* The other

pleads to all who pass
*Help her, girlie, help her, young woman,
help her, mister.*

My aunt murmurs back
in Sicilian no one understands.
What looks through those "dead-looking"

eyes my cousin hates, what
sees the elevator, what thinks
it's talking to the prince's ghost?

GHOST VOLCANO

My love, my dead one, is it a seed, a stone,
a jagged tooth that goes on wanting, and wanting
to go on?

        All night,
while her daughter disinfects its "nighties"
down the road, the black soup closes

over its head.
        All night,
tied to a bed in room 24,

it screeches *mama, mama.*

June 15, 1992: Widow's Walk, Harpswell, Maine

A moon like a bloody animal eye over the inlet,
low, low toward the hill as if struggling
to cool itself in the chill black salt of the mudflats;
and the salt stench of the marshes simmers around
the tipsy wharf I walk on.

My dear,
I ate what I was told to try—
tonight chowder, lobster, sweet corn
and a blueberry muffin; last night clams
and lobster, steamed, baked, stewed.

Yesterday Joanne and I wandered through Bath,
admiring the white and black whalers' mansions,
the widow's walks where stoic wives
paced with straining eyes, scanning the long
flat sea for specks of motion.

And I sucked in the light flung out by the sea
at Popham Beach, drank up the buckets of salt wind
shifting the pale New England sands.
I'm stuffed with this state where we summered
thirty years ago.

Remember
the cabin on Frenchman's Bay,
swelled with our secret heat, under the covers,
while bats flapped through the pines
and moths banged on the screens?

That's how I feel:
bloated with love
too heavy to hold, fat as the past.
The wharf rocks with the weight
of what I carry—

GHOST VOLCANO

myself and you,
too much for one scared woman,
yet I'm looking for more,
pacing and looking,
as if any minute now,

in the lingering blue of almost solstice,
the old tour boat might sputter up to me,
me and you at the rails,
squinting against the sun
and eager for souvenirs.

IV

NOTES ON MASADA

▲ ▲ ▲

... at the very moment when with streaming eyes they
embraced and caressed their wives, and taking their children
in their arms pressed upon them the last, lingering kisses,
hands other than their own seemed to assist them and they
carried out their purpose ... and when ten of them had been
chosen by lot to be the executioners of the rest, every man
lay down beside his wife and children where they lay, flung
his arms round them, and exposed his throat to those who
must perform the painful office. These unflinchingly
slaughtered them all, then agreed on the same rule for each
other, so that the one who drew the lot should kill the nine
and last of all himself: such perfect confidence they all had
in each other that neither in doing nor in suffering would
one differ from another. . . . but an old woman escaped,
along with another ... in intelligence and education superior
to most women, and five little children. They had hidden in
the conduits that brought drinking water underground while
the rest were intent upon the suicide pact. These numbered
960, women and children included.

—Josephus, The Jewish War

Notes on Masada

—for Elliot in 1990, with love and thanks to Shirley Kaufman and Bill Daleski

1.

All night, every night, those old stones,
the color of heat,
stand on the mountain, centuries gusting past,

and the plain is still the same: the Dead Sea
glistening its vitreous salts between
opposing walls of silence,

the rings of squared-off Roman camps
etched into a low plateau.
Jammed with Japanese sightseers,

the cable car heaves us
above circling hawks and
Herod's northern palace. It's almost noon

and the desert sun
scours every crevice clean.
You tell me this dry pure air

preserved the holy scrolls at Qumran.
Isaiah, scribbled in the wilderness,
and unknown psalms.

When we scramble to the peak, I almost
fear to find the last ten zealots facing me,
their parchment fingers

gripping blood-starved blades, their bodies
plunged like stakes across the path
to bar our passage

toward the crumbling synagogue.

GHOST VOLCANO

2.

In a battered Volvo, driving through the German Colony
on the way to Mea Shearim—place of "100 gates"—
Malka said: *Do you belong to a synagogue?*

"I'm not Jewish, but maybe through my father's father. . . ."
I answered, offering tales of a tattered
coat of arms, a Renaissance Star of David.

"That won't do any good," she said
in the kindest way.
I know. I know a Jew must be born

from the mother, from the bloody
flesh: the zealots wouldn't
have bothered to strike me dead—would they?—

at the hot top of Masada.

3.

We poke through the 2000-year-old storerooms.
Here were the amphorae holding oil and grain.
Here were the pomegranate seeds the archaeologist

sought to remember and restore. What
loincloths, headdresses, Bedouin
shawls did they wear, as

the golden Roman sun shone down
daily, daily?
The lines of shadow

cast across the desert
are vertiginously perpendicular,
the angles of a cross,

or of crossed swords.

4.

I confess: I hate religion.
The six sects of the Holy Sepulchre.
We descended into the pink marble tomb.

You told me to light a candle.
I crossed myself, spurious, and "prayed."
"Mass psychosis," I complained, hovering

next to Israeli honeysuckle, breathing
hyssop and cinnamon.
                              Our grandchild,

someone says, looks like an angel.
Botticelli. But angels are circumcised,
know what they are for. And he isn't,

and we don't.

5.

The head of the eggplant cracks open.
Purple turns golden.
Royal vegetable. And *hummus*. And *tahina*.

"Why must the Jews eat like Arabs?
Aren't you at war with the Arabs?"
White shrouds on their heads, gold

abstraction in the mosques, sky-
blue hieroglyphs, no matter
where we go. And stones.

And stones.

6.

We quarrel in our California kitchen, eating porkchops
and frozen creamed potatoes.
Out of nowhere and for nothing

I say the dreaded Christian thing:
What made those old priests want to murder
that young one? (And you—do I mean to say

are you their heir?)
You're apoplectic. I've never seen
your face so red and startled.

You didn't do it. You shouldn't have married me.

7.

By the Dead Sea, its turquoise scales
splitting like the belly of an Egyptian fish,
we bow to the sun and the sacred mud.

We're in the casual
solarium where psoriatics
come to suffer, be cured.

Naked women and men reveal their
terrible scabs; they lie
like Hans Castorp in the

midday heat: it will be
all right they say—they're Swiss
and German, Scandinavian and

English: *okeh, okeh.*
"You see how well he's done," notes one Israeli
technician: "Look at his elbows,"

look at his healing dinosaur
scales. He's native,
he's Jewish. I'm not.

Can I be cured?

8.

I'm not who I am. Bless you!
In Mea Shearim, the signs tell me so:
Jewish Daughter: Keep Your Clothing Modest.

100 Gates. The men wear black
satin bathrobes, white knee
breeches, furry cossack hats.

Do I want them to love me? Do I want
their prayers to purify my *goyische* body?
Their hands, their pale intentions, shut the gates against me.

What I call my "faith" is crippled and poor.

9.

Beyond the archaic bathhouse, the storage room, the
synagogue, hectic aquas sing
the Dead Sea's mysteries:

how Vespasian's prisoners,
"hands tied behind them in deep water,"
rose to the surface

"as if blown upwards by a strong wind,"
how Josephus saw black lumps of asphalt
floating past "like headless bulls."

I see blank light, bare heat.
The Roman legions came and did not conquer.
At a wedding outside Tel Aviv last week

I watched a famous "textual" critic learning
a Sephardic hora.
My words on this page

are as equivocal as his steps.

GHOST VOLCANO

10.

And what about the mysteries of Cana?
Grandma and Grandpa
stare like icons from a gold-rimmed photograph.

An eighteen-year-old Russian governess,
Grandma rode a camel in Egypt, 1900, then in 1973
bequeathed her Arab souvenirs to me. Me!

I cross myself as if stammering,
"Did you kill—
                    who did *you* kill?"

and heat infuses us, heat
leaps like a headless bull
out of the seething glitter.

If we could drown this heat in the flat
Dead Sea. Heat of the cross
and the burned-out bush.

Heat of the two women and the five children
in the magic cistern.
Heat of the nine hundred sixty killed

and the ten killers.

11.

What about, as our son put it, *the absolute
hopelessness of the whole
human endeavor?*

Did the bones of my Lord
rise in the Church of the Holy
Sepulchre? Pink stone, a hundred lamps

swaying over tourist hairdos. Crazed
old ladies with shawls or permanents.
Incense fumes.

One shekel for a candle.
I hear our Berkeley daughter say
Religion sucks—

but the genuflecting worshippers
drink this acid thirstily, the six
processions warring over holidays, the palms

with sword-sharp edges.
Kill us, they implore, *in the Holy Land.
We must die together*

under this magnificent desolate sky.

GHOST VOLCANO

12.

The shadows of the Church
slam down around me
like the walls of the sacred tomb.

The Israeli archaeologist digs into the
sand of Masada,
he plants a pomegranate

in the courtyard of the columbarium
where holy doves once fluttered
and were roasted.

A new emptiness cracks open.
Am I a Jew? And who killed Christ?
On the day after *Shabbat* the Council of Torah Sages

wrestles with the words of the aged rabbi in Brooklyn,
as a wind from the Dead Sea
hisses across Masada, threatening

like a terrorist: "I'll flay you alive,
hang you up for the jackals!"
And in the dingy

Chapel of the Resurrection, the guardian
Russian monk is blank as a hothouse camellia.
His hundred lamps halo the scabrous

stones like wishes for health.

13.

Mount Scopus. A lavish lunch at the university.
Deans and provosts. They gossip with each other
in unintelligible Hebrew. Smiling,

they query me in English. The red-bearded man
on my right, they say, is "the world's
greatest Biblical scholar."

Over dense pot roast and *risotto,*
he tells me his theory:
It was the desert, the people

of the desert,
who "invented" monotheism.
Here, he argues,

there is one sky, one glaring
sky, the cyclops eye of a
single Yahweh,

and only that. No
little gods of the grove, no rivulets
or idols. Only the sky.

Should my tiny self, with its yearnings,
trickle away? Shall I enter
the hundred shuttered gates?

Lunch lapses into silence. The dean coughs.
We sip communal wine.
I think, "Elliot, your name is really *Elijah*—"

Eliahu: I wish I could leave this wine in a cup for you!
But you're laughing and telling jokes,
while outside the university window

GHOST VOLCANO

a vicious blue,
keen and intransigent as Dead Sea salt,
sinks further into itself.

I imagine that century by century,
horrifying as the top of Masada,
the caves toward which they crawled

—prickly hutches for the scrolls, the bones,
the unimaginable abstract
bits of sword and crucifix—

sucked up that blue.

V

WIDOW'S WALK

▲   ▲   ▲

September 5, 1992: New Hampshire, under the Woods

Under the tall woods as if under sea,
under the breezy dapple you'd have loved, under

the tide of light that moves the birds from sky to tree
and off and up again, and under

the butterfly float of leafy hands
just letting go, just calmly airily

relinquishing the branches where they grew,
under the motion, the breathing, the wise

and prudent sway of stalks that bow and yield
to rise again, under the silence

that trills for hours, under the messages
that shift from cloud to cloud,

I hunch on my porch, walled in
by rusty screens, dead boards, gray paint.

Am I the only unchanging thing?
Almost nineteen months without you, and I can't

let go, can't drift like some dumb
leaf away and off:
                          instead it looks as though
the grimy ratio that governs me—

you fixed down there / me stuck up here—
was centuries ago

engraved in stone
by Plato.

September 7, 1992: Labor Day in the Woods, outside Peterborough

Today, strange whirrings in the *selva oscura*:
birds in the ferns? the fox in her lair? a flock
of insects revving up?
                                        Another

animal, I crack through brambles, crunch
leaves, needles—the long deep
floor of the past, and wonder
am I here, or where, or lost . . .

I've slept all day, watched all night:
my sense of time's not right—
and hiking deeper into the prickly green, the shadow,
I drag you too,

                        although you still
refuse to answer, even signal.
It's as if I hauled a sledge of granite,
smashing into birches, crushing berry bushes,

over and over, hour after hour, turning
and flinging my body onto the dead
load of the stone body
in the hope that here, if anywhere,

among the stirrings of the forest,
I might breathe on you,
                                        breathe love or panic,
and like some keen laborious god

induce the stone to speak.

September 10, 1992: Picking Wildflowers
in New Hampshire

Wading through the meadow, a Keatsian
cloud of "small gnats swarming" round me,
a continuo of crickets underfoot,
I choose these few sparse blossoms
for my desk and in your memory.

You'd love, I know, the cottage in the pines
where this month I moon my days away, half-napping,
half-scribbling half-formed tales of you
and me and how you lived and why
you died,

        and love, I think, the sudden
furtive spears of goldenrod just thrusting up
along the winding road that rims this field,
the dense coarse grass I'm walking on, the line
of evergreens that walls each space I move in.

You'd love! I hate the phrase, I hate that bleak
subjunctive, never ending, always postulating
the impossible.
        What *would* you love, what *can* I love,
in the empty meadow, the unpeopled house?

And yet my grammar acquiesces, helpless.
Here's what you'd say, I tell myself.
You'd say:
        Look at these nameless wildflowers,
their skinny stems as tough as rubber bands,

their tiny leaves and petals opened just enough,
enough to suit their needs and the needs
of the DNA.
            They're economical,
they live on almost nothing.

If you have to, so can you.

November 26, 1992: Thanksgiving at the Sea Ranch, Contemplating Metempsychosis

You tried coming back as a spider.
I was too fast for you. As you
climbed my ankle, I swept you off, I ground you

to powder under my winter boot.
Shall I cherish the black widow,
I asked, because he is you?

You were cunning: you became
the young, the darkly masked
raccoon that haunts my deck.

Each night for weeks you tiptoed
toward the sliding doors, your paws
imploring, eyes aglow. *Let me in,*

Let me back in, you hissed,
swaying beside the tubbed fuchsia,
shadowing the fancy cabbage in its Aztec pot.

And you've been creatures of the air and sea,
the hawk that sees into my skull, the seal that barks
a few yards from the picnic on the shore.

Today you chose a different life, today
you're trying to stumble
through the tons of dirt that hold you down:

you're a little grove of mushrooms,
rising from the forest floor you loved.
Bob saw you in the windbreak—

November mushrooms, he said,
off-white and probably poisonous.
Shall I slice you for the feast?

If I eat you will I die back into your arms?
Shall I give thanks for God's wonders
because they all are you, and you are them?

The meadow's silent, its dead grasses
ignore each other and the evening walkers
who trample them. What will you be,

I wonder, when the night wind rises?
Come back as yourself, in your blue parka,
your plaid flannel shirt with the missing button.

These fields that hum and churn with life
are empty. There is nowhere
you are not, nowhere

you are not not.

VI

WATER MUSIC

Water Music

1. The Nature of Water

First, the clarity, those
molecules you go through and through,
and through you they go

in the long sift of blood.
And the shine goes through
as if something—you?—believes

in color, something stipulates
now blue, now what's called
green or black. You think

you might name it *landscape*,
but it's that utter
clearness, giving up

all ideas except reflection.
And then the changes, loose
and free to stiff, stiff

and still to shapeless
spirit of shape.
Do you bend today by the stream

that swivels through you?
Does it mark its currents on your skin?
Kneel in the rain and crook your fingers:

look! clear and changing
every minute
asteroids of still or shapeless

drip from your rosy
nails, and swarming and cold and clear
they're the only halo around

the head you think
so lovable, so
venerable.

2. The Water Goddess

They said they found her in the cabbage
core, pale green, her skin

a film of lived
invisibility. They

asked what was she,
what and who?

Only a humble
female infiltration, a

kind of mouse
or insect,

nibbling at the roots?
Then the flaring, then the odd

drenching, the permeation:
she lifted salt,

streaked toward taste
and up

and up
into the veins

of bland and stupid leaf
until she was what they wanted

(or wanted to define)
as no producer but a

product, warm
and sincere, albeit thin—

a kind of soup or broth?
an odd embarrassed heat?

She had her purposes
(they thought).

GHOST VOLCANO

3. The Character of Water

It happens inside the grape,
between those thin im-
permeable green walls:

it sweetens
suddenly, as if the sea
were tamed, lay flat yet

rounded, rounding: yes,
it's passive, daring
nothing

as it grows and heaps itself
into a gel that clots
the tongue with wonder.

What's liquid in you reaches
forward, stunned that salt
and bitter

could change to heavy
smooth, and it opens
as you open

sucking you down lanes
of spring—past peaches, weeds,
cows in a grassy field.

Remember this, remember
how the churn of silence
labors in you as you

gasp and open to it
breathing out
and in the April pasture,

orchard, vineyard
where an ocean edge
declaims your origin.

Maine and the spinning
sailboats! Vera
Cruz and the flying fish!

Everywhere
the air is dense
with roots of water

wishing to convince your
every lacy cell
that you're turning into sugar.

4. The Ice Cubes

So: here's nature and culture—
in fact, little
windows of steel, jail

cells where water sits
immobilized and purified
as if beaten into its own

dead center. But then,
who are the lunatics, the hopeful
vandals who'd fill

such clarity
with violets or cyclamens?
Softness would shrivel

in the iron tray,
where suddenly everything's
geometrical. *If I'm a*

cube, you must be a
cube too, each says to the other,
sweating droplets onto

the barriers, weeping
slivers of itself
into the straight stern lanes

of *real* solid
that refuse to let go of all
this frozen energy, this will

to flow and flow.
Let us go
out of shape, the cubes demand,

out of exquisite
ache, out of Plato's arrogant
mind, out of

humiliating Euclid.

5. Hard Water

stifling the pipes,
and that blue mean
taste on the tongue,

tang of the difficult
elements, each
asserting its own

will to endure, to be
known: keen
thin iron

in the mouth—and swallowed
filling the innocent
back of the throat,

the gullet that only wants
air and sweet and milky
in tender sips.

So hard you find its white
shadow in the tub,
a film of stone

grown in the hollow
where you were dumb enough
to let your body lie.

A film, a stain.
And veil on veil, the foreign
molecules insist on

clinging to their place.
Your place.
Every night when you rise

shiny from the bath,
your softness chilling
as comfort spills and pools

on the cold floor,
you try to scrub that
stain away.

Every morning the film
has thickened, where
all night the tap

dripped and toppled its hard
water into the same
roughening spot.

GHOST VOLCANO

6. Brine

Instead of sweet or neutral,
instead of leafy,
instead of air,
instead of the long stream of light,
instead of the quick stitches of wind
fastening and loosening warmth,

the great wave comes over,
the mouth of bitterness opens,
the muscles of the deep
gut of salt
clench, the belly
of cold distends,

and you are taken in,
into the cave where
salt and bitter
are needles piercing your skin,
tiny knives writing their names
in every cell.

On some shore, some
mythical solid,
the water that falls
falls like the sort of goodness
Plato propounded—
and others are watching you there,

they believe in the blades of change,
they preach the archaic
doctrine of brine as womb,
while you spin through
the blistering gray
that spins through your eyes.

Sandra M. Gilbert

Hold your breath.
Don't tell them
the truth of the brine.
Be dull, be dumb.
Pretend you're a stone
in a kindly pond.

Don't ever let yourself name
the bitter that prints its name
in your blood.
Don't even let yourself taste
the buds of salt
that are tasting you.

7. The Water Table

It rises in darkness, indifferent,
rotting the dead and complicating roots.

It doesn't know it's there.
It doesn't know it is.

It knows it wants to spread,
to be level, to be everywhere.

It wants to enter everything,
it wants what happens to happen,

wants to be drawn upward,
to be lifted past the thick, the black,

into sheets of light,
to glitter in that light,

to devour the light
and sink again

into its own flatness,
its imperviousness.

And you—
you think you dine at the table of water

as shooting stars dine on the universe.

8. The Lake

is said to be the deepest in Europe.
Beyond Milan, the granite carbuncles,

the vast stiff lace they call the Duomo,
it goes greenly blackly down,

the cold inside it traveling as low
as the Swiss Diavolezza reaches high.

The twitch of minnows near the gravelly shore,
the punctuating snakes,

refuse to fall that far, where
flaccid dark meets muscle of ice.

Is it China, as the children think?
Is it a mind that has no bottom?

It is the opposite of all we believe.
It is the other side of the shriek of a bird or the scream of a cat.

The blank massifs stare into it.
Although Pliny and Serbelloni have come and gone

and these (the brooding walker says) remain,
they too will sag, draggle—

caduta massi!—
and erode into the viscous fluid

where groaning ferries float
like tiny cakes of light,

offering themselves to the dead.

9. Rain

In the night,
an immense seething through the trees,
a seething and hissing as of a hasty invasion
led by brilliant insects from the north,

and then a scratching a tearing
a sudden scarification of windows, a plunge
of something swift and shapeless
and impartial

into leaves dirt stones shells flesh,
a flashing without color
into color. . . .
In the kitchen garden

the shriveled petals of the pelargonium
tremble and are smashed,
the roots of carrots, cabbages,
dilate and reach and suck and rot.

And you who nod beside the reading lamp,
seeing in a drowned half-sleep
only the pink of your fingers
as they cling to the edges of this page,

have you heard that seething from the sky?
By the time you wake,
shake yourself,
and rise to close the blinds,

it is over and it is calm, calm
and over.

VII

WIDOW'S WALK

March 14, 1993: Berkeley:
Trying Not to Think of a White Bear

When he was naughty, Tolstoy's brothers told little Leo he would
be forgiven if he could stand in a corner for five minutes and not
think of a white bear.

I tried. Ten seconds maybe, that was all—
but she was coming toward me, sailing, rather,
on a cake of ice high as a house, her white fur
shining like the midnight sun.

Can we not, said one friend,
exorcise the referential?
The words "white" and "bear" are merely sounds,
they need not signify.

I tried. Five more seconds.
This time I could see her claws:
steely hooks, I thought,
the size of picture hangers,

and she was twice my height, and as she moved
I noted lice or fleas, jumpy commas,
troubling her pelt so that the fine hairs
flipped and flicked.

De dictu, said another friend, *de rerum.*
An ancient problem.
I say "white" and "bear,"
and I see only letters.

She kept on coming, now so close
I sniffed her fishy whiskers, looked up
into her small flat sorrowful thoughtless
winter-sunset eyes.

From somewhere in the center of her twitching,
a humming rose, a growl like cellos
tuning up or like that one deep note
in *Rheingold* where the world begins.

Nomians versus antinomians, a third explained.
An old debate—but
perhaps you wouldn't be you if
you could not think of a white bear.

Her iceberg towers. Glistens. Upright, keening,
she rides it toward me just the way Brunhilde
straddled Grania, galloping toward Siegfried,
the way Isolde, motionless,

rode the prow of her ship toward Lyonesse
where Tristan lay.
                    My love,
you're dead at her feet—

dead, I mean, between her giant paws—
swaddled in your faded parka.
                              No,
you're swimming, brisk and rosy, in the Arctic

green around, your frosty beard
gleaming like her fur, your eyes
that same flat sunset color.
                            No, you're

standing near her, standing
in her great pale shadow
on that slippery cliff of ice, keening and smiling
and gliding toward me over and over.

I can't not think of a white bear
the way I can't not think of you.

March 22, 1993: Puerto Vallarta, Sierra Madre / Baya de Los Banderos

Not clouds, mountains. A slow wall
humped and blue, a goddess arm
embracing the bay, cold-shouldering
the green shrieks of the valleys.

Not clouds, mountains. But vague
as clouds, fingering distances the way
clouds do, propounding the invisible
like clouds—and blue and solemn.

Sierra madre, mother mountain,
sealing off the past, the humid
plazas where we swooped like swallows,
the glimmering swamps we loved and where we loved.

Gone, says the *madre*, wise
in her humped silence, *Never
to be seen again. Hidden
behind my clefts and wonders.*

Not clouds, mountains,
she is solid, stony,
stolid as coffins.
Not clouds, mountains, she recommends

the enormous yawn of the sea.

Spring Equinox, 1993: Puerto Vallarta, Playa de Los Muertos

Nearer and nearer the Equator, nearer
the tropic of impossibles where
leaves don't die and blossoms

the size of paradise
open celestial jaws and on
the *playa de los muertos*

the dead are bathing, complacent,
in a sun of every color, they are
bathing in our memory of them:

they've forgotten to fear
their death, they've long forgotten
to fear their lives, and now

they bask, they almost smile, they
wait. Now and then
one remembers the reason—

the *wish*, the *walk*, the *swim*:
but it's hard to walk without
the drag of the body, to swim

without the flesh that rises on the curve
of every wave, hard to wish
without blood or nerve.

                         That's why
they need us, *you* need *me*:
to walk, to wish.

You don't know, I guess, but now,
right now, I'm watching you,
watching as you strive to rise,

GHOST VOLCANO

watching as you stumble
to the rim of salt, the waterline.
And see, my love

walks you across the border,
urges the wish, teaches the swim.
Camped on my own hot shore,

I send you forth—you deeply burning
in yourself like a floating candle,
you musing and lit with your own past—

I send you like a hieroglyph or a letter
to God, across the shining gulf,
toward the unimaginable ice cliffs

south of the south.

VIII

CALLA LILIES

▲   ▲   ▲

Calla Lilies

Stacked in banks of cream, pale foreigners,
they crane their long green necks, green bodies,
over irises, wild grasses, poppies,
calm and only mildly startled
by the light that quakes across the sky.

Down there, in the *before*,
everything was closed: what moved
moved inside the seals, the fastenings,
the enormous heaviness through which
from time to time
small stirrings crept.

                          But then the stones
softened, the gates of the cold unlocked.
Something began to lift them, something began
a steep crawl up the slope of shadow.

Now, bland and open in their bridal satin,
they extrude gold tongues, gold phalluses
into a warmth that loves them back,
and sway and bow in the Easter breeze.

Imperturbable as cream,
they have forgotten the wrists and ribs of the dead
from whose pallets they have risen.

IX

WIDOW'S WALK

▲   ▲   ▲

December 1, 1993: Paris, Looking at Monet

No wonder Monet's yellow irises
spurt from the pit below the picture,
jets of heat crazy for air, swerving
toward light, toward fire.

Three-quarters of a century ago
they flung themselves in front of him,
forced their petals, tossing and golden,
through Giverny's purple veils, its blue disguises

into the Marmottan—
and a little more than a decade later
you appeared, you too so starved for light
you howled like every man

as something tore you from that pit
between your mother's thighs.
Today would be your birthday—sixty-three!—
and thirty-six years

since we pledged ourselves,
swearing a troth or truth
we didn't truly understand
but really—so I see it now—

marrying the opposite of all that
emptiness those blind and yearning
irises despise.
What kept us drifting forward

as a century's sluice of dark
unfurled, unscrolled?
Our thoughts cloaked the surface of shadow
like that painter's water lilies,

breathing in light as if at any
agitation of the stream
we two, we too, might be dragged down,
down and back.

February 11, 1994: Berkeley, Anniversary Waltz Again

The year revolves toward pink and red,
toward the tiny Valentine
hearts of the plums,

each blossom a pink frill
and a core of blood, a frill
and its bloody core. . . .

Three times the nurses wheeled you into the icy room,
three-quarters of your life just barely over.
Three years since you set out for nowhere,

three years I've studied these blossoms alone,
the indifferent flush, the roseate
aplomb they set against bare blue.

To have gone on becoming without you!
Three nights now since we met in sleep,
and I told you sorrowfully

that you were dead—
three nights since you wept in rage,
lifted your handsome shadowy head and howled.

But how your face has changed!
You're beardless and pale,
a different man, a *spirit* man,

as if when we were spun away from each other,
as if when I took my first three giant steps
into another somewhere,

you too could never be the same,
you too had to go on becoming
and becoming other,

becoming alone. . . .
As if the only February thing
that's sure to be the same

is still the plum tree's
blind pink three-week waltz
with air and light and darkness.

February 14, 1994: At the Point Reyes Lighthouse

On the edge of the intelligible:
the long blind toneless hum
of the signal the rock-walled

lighthouse won't stop sending out,
the almost unheard "moaning"—
so the rangers call it—

of the huddled colony of murres,
the intermittent spout and froth
of gray whales journeying north,

the nearly blinding glitter of sunlight
sharpening its thousand knives,
against the hiss and blather of the waves. . . .

And you are still stopped dead.

Below the air you lie, away from the balm,
under the clipped lawn
in your good jacket, your fancy tie.

Shattering silence here and there,
the great whales pulse and spume
beneath the lighthouse's warning hum. . . .

The film of their breathing
flaps banners of bitter
joy in the salty wind.